# TIME TO GET STARTED

First published 2008 by
Procedor Publications

CIP catalogue records for this book are available from the British Library.

ISBN 978-0-9559216-0-5

**Procedor Publications**
Suite 14
35 George Street
London W1U 3QP

Design by Heidi B Thorsen

Printed and bound in the UK by
Cromwell Press Limited, Trowbridge, Wiltshire.

To my father
Forrest Fritz

# TIME TO GET *started*

## CHAPTERS

# TIME TO GET *started*

It is my moral duty to start this foreword with a warning: Mark Fritz's punchy bite-sized chunks of wisdom are highly addictive.

I write as an addict.

I first noticed the addiction while watching my daughters play tennis on Saturday mornings. When they were settled in I would switch my focus to the Blackberry to study the seven gems that Mark had emailed for the week. At the time I was in the process of setting up my new company – so handy hints and inspiration were especially welcome. But sometimes as the tennis got underway the tips were yet to arrive. It was then I realised my addiction. I would keep diving back into the Blackberry as the lessons progressed until they duly appeared. I would then be satisfied for another week – until the craving returned.

Now that Mark has collected the highlights of his profound thoughts into a single volume, addicts won't have to wait from week to week. And having received an advance copy, I have been able to scoff the tips with undignified gluttony.

In the wake of this overdose, I don't know what will happen next. Though I suspect that if I can put all Mark's advice into action it might, just might, ward off the craving for more.

What I've tried to apply so far has certainly worked with aplomb.

One of the reasons Mark's tips are so addictive is that they often tell you what you inherently know. But they are conveyed with such clarity and succinctness, that you might have struggled to express the thought in such a powerful way to yourself.

There are other tips that have taken me by surprise. One that has stuck most in my mind concerned what to do when a new problem strikes. I've found Mark's advice, 'what's the best thing about this problem?', to be a compelling way of switching into a more positive mode of thinking, at a time when the natural tendency is to do the opposite.

Having scrutinized all the tips in this book, there is one thing which I find particularly uncanny – I can't find anything with which I disagree. As a broadcast journalist and media trainer schooled in the art of playing devil's advocate to any proposition, this is truly shocking.

But there's an inherent natural logic that underpins Mark's thoughts, which makes arguing with them difficult. This is part of their charm – and their effectiveness.

And as someone who is constantly striving to get myself and others to communicate in impactive, pithy parcels of information, I cannot help but admire the artistry involved in getting each potentially life-changing thought into a headline and a few short sentences.

There is a popular BBC programme which invites guests to imagine they are stranded on a desert island – and only permitted a few possessions including a single book (excluding for some reason The Bible and the Complete Works of Shakespeare).

If readers find themselves in such a situation – either on the show or on a real desert island – then this book would be hard to go past.

It doesn't tell you precisely how to build a vessel to escape the island. But it would give you inspiration for the ideas and the get-up-and-go required to put your plans into action.

Happy sailing.

And if you find yourself becoming an addict too, then just ask yourself: 'What's the best thing about this addiction?' The answers will be all around you.

# TIME TO GET *started*

## WELCOME TO THE BOOK...

*Time to Get Started* is a compilation of the best thoughts from the first two years of *Mark Fritz's Daily Thoughts* (www.procedor.com/daily-thought.html)

The goal below says it all about the focus of this book.

## THE GOAL
**TO PROVIDE ➜ THOUGHTS TO INSPIRE ACTION IN YOU**

The thoughts are grouped together (five per page) by a theme, along with a related quote and a take-away to inspire you to think and act.

This is great book to use for your daily inspiration, as you can use the table of contents to get some inspiration on a specific theme that is on your mind that particular day.

## ONE HINT
As you read through each theme, move forward to the next page only after you have asked yourself the following question: 'How do I apply this to my own life?'

This is the first and most important action you can take while reading this book. Asking yourself 'How do I apply this to my own life?' moves you to thinking about the possible action you can take.

Very often we read books and say to ourselves, 'That's interesting.' However, if we keep our thoughts at only a 'That's interesting' level, we never get to thinking about the Action we can take from what we learned.

When we move from 'That's interesting' to 'How do I apply this?', we start to make changes in our lives.

Why? When we think about how we can apply the learning, we are thinking in an 'Action Mode' and basically wiring our brain for action. The next time a situation comes where we could possibly use this learning, our brain then serves it up to us.

Remember, after each theme – ask yourself:
HOW DO I APPLY THIS TO MY OWN LIFE?

## DESIGN A LIFE – NOT MAKE A LIVING

If you really want to be the best you can be, you need to think about designing a life and not just making a living. Just making a living doesn't have enough power to drive you to be the best you can be. So, start today and design the life you want first, and then begin taking action to become the person who will then get it.

## MANAGE YOUR LIFE, OR YOUR LIFE MANAGES YOU

Too many people today let their life manage them. They let others and circumstances drive what they feel and do in their lives, and usually because they do not have goals that could guide them to make the right choices on how they could use their time. Do you have goals that could help you make the right choices, or are you letting your life manage you?

## LIFE IS A GAME OF CHOICE, NOT CHANCE

There is a huge difference between successful and unsuccessful people. Successful people have a focus that guides the choices they make (from how they use their time, to who is most important to them). Unsuccessful people have little focus and leave everything in their life up to chance. Remember, your focus guides your choices, and your choices create your life.

## LIVE BY WHAT YOU BELIEVE VS. WHAT YOU FEEL

Successful people start off each day believing that they will do well in whatever they do that day. They might not always feel their best (either physically or mentally), but that belief in their success is always there. Develop the belief in yourself and then live by it.

## A LIFE LIVED WELL IS A BALANCING ACT

We have all seen people who have created successful businesses suddenly burn out. They put so much of themselves into their business that they have nothing left for anything else. Truly successful people understand that a life lived well is a continual balancing act. They keep all the key elements of their life in focus and make sure they keep the balance.

Destiny is not a matter of chance, it is a matter of choice; it is not a thing to be waited for, it is a thing to be achieved.

*William Jennings Bryan*

LIFE IS A
CHOICE
MADE BY YOU
OR OTHERS

CHOOSE
FOR YOURSELF

TIME TO GET
*started*

## THE IMPORTANCE OF 'WHY'

There's a very good quote that goes like this: 'You can take almost any How, as long as you have a big enough Why.' That is so very true. When we really know why we want something (building a very strong need for it), then we do almost anything to make it happen. If you have a goal or a project that isn't moving as fast as you would like, a good place to start is to ask yourself, 'Why is this important to me?' Probably, you will find that your 'Why' is not as strong as you originally thought. Build a strong 'Why' and you can do almost anything.

## SELL YOURSELF TO YOURSELF FIRST

Before you can sell yourself and your abilities to others, you need to sell yourself to yourself first. Affirmations are a good way of reinforcing the good things in yourself and what you can accomplish – and have accomplished. Practise affirmations daily, and you will begin to sell yourself to others in a much more powerful way.

## MEETING OUR NEEDS DOESN'T HAVE ENOUGH POWER

You often hear people say, "If only I can make enough money to..." Just meeting our needs is not really powerful enough. It doesn't get us excited or create the right energy to make things happen. It is important to define goals that inspire us and create the energy and excitement to fuel the necessary action. Create some exciting goals today.

## BE CLEAR ON WHAT YOU WANT AND WHY

Clarity should be a key word for everyone, as we all need to be clear on what we want. However, this alone is not enough. We also need to understand why we want it. A strong 'Why' provides the drive and energy to have us do whatever it takes to get what we want. Take the time to be clear on the 'What' and the 'Why', and it will not be long until you get what you want.

## CONTINUE TO REPLAY THE 'WHY'

For every goal we create, we will always encounter challenges on our way to that goal. What will keep you positive in meeting those challenges, is constantly to replay the 'Why' behind what you want to achieve. Remember, a big 'Why' can take almost any 'How'.

He who has a 'why' to live can bear with almost any 'how'.

*Friedrich Nietzsche*

BUILD YOUR
WHY

TO BUILD THE
POWER
BEHIND YOUR
HOW

## ATTITUDE ACTIVATES EVERYTHING ELSE

I heard an interesting saying the other day: 'All things being equal, attitude wins. All things not being equal, attitude sometimes still wins.' Our attitude often speaks to people louder than what we say or the skills that we have. A great attitude is what activates everything else; it provides the fuel to take action, and taking action is what separates successful people from unsuccessful people. Think about how your attitude is each day. Think about the people you meet and what differences there may be if you keep a different attitude.

## TAKE RESPONSIBILITY FOR YOUR OWN ATTITUDE

Many times you will hear people say, 'He or she doesn't make me happy.' These people are always relying on others to help them stay happy. However, their attitude is not another's responsibility, but their own. When people take responsibility for their own attitude (happiness), they begin to act in a way that drives people to act differently around them. Remember: take responsibility for your own attitude.

## YOUR ATTITUDE WON'T TAKE CARE OF ITSELF

Your attitude will never stay positive unless you continually feed it with positive and inspiring messages. These positive messages come from being around other positive people, reading books that will inspire and energise you, listening to inspiring speakers, etc. Feed your attitude daily to keep it positive.

## ATTITUDE IS NOT DEPENDENT ON CIRCUMSTANCES

Many people set their attitude based on how others treat them during the day. They are letting outside circumstances decide how they want to live the day. Attitude is not an outside thing. We all need to determine our attitude before the day hits us, and why not decide to have a good one from the very beginning of the day?

## BECOME THE PERSON YOU WOULD WANT TO BE AROUND

I think we would all act a little differently if we acted like the person we would want to be around. How often do we put ourselves in a negative mood because our day didn't go the way we had planned? Would we want to be around ourselves on that day? Probably not! Become the person you would want to be around, all the time.

Your attitude determines
your altitude!
*Denis Waitley*

YOUR ATTITUDE
DRIVES YOUR
SUCCESS

EITHER
FORWARDS
OR BACKWARDS

TIME TO GET *started*

## HAVE GOALS IN ALL PARTS OF YOUR LIFE

People very often establish goals for their work life, but forget to set goals for their private life as well. We all need to drive a balanced life, and that means having balanced goals. Take a few minutes to review your goals and make sure you have a balanced approach.

## YOUR GOALS SHOULD BOTH SCARE AND EXCITE YOU

There is a very good way to see if you are setting the right goals. Basically, your goals should both scare and excite you at the same time. Why? Because the big goals are the ones that challenge us to grow in order to meet them. That scares us, but almost always motivates us to try the impossible.

## THE TARGET YOU DO NOT HAVE

I am reminded of the quote from Zig Ziglar: "You cannot hit a target you do not have." Many people can talk for 10 minutes on all the things they do not want, but struggle to define clearly what they do want – their targets. Successful people know clearly what they want; they have their targets, and take action on them. It is much more motivating to take action towards a target, than trying to avoid those things we do not want. So, why not define your targets today?

## A GOAL MEANS CHANGE

It is so important when defining a goal also to define right away all the changes that need to be made in order to achieve that goal. Remember, you are not committed to the goal unless you are committed to the changes necessary to achieve that goal. Therefore, when you define your next goal, define the changes at the same time.

## GOALS WORTHY OF YOUR TALENTS

Most people don't have the success they would like in life because they set too low a target for their life. They either lack goals or are really setting goals that are not challenging them at all. They are not setting goals worthy of their talents. How about you? Are your goals truly worthy of your talents?

Big goals get big results.
No goals gets no results
or somebody else's results.
*Mark Victor Hansen*

# GOALS
## SET BOTH THE
# DIRECTION

# AND PACE
## OF YOUR OWN
# SUCCESS

## MOVE YOUR VOCABULARY FROM 'TRY' TO 'DO'

Too often we respond to a request with the words: 'I will try to do it by then.' 'Try' is such a vague word and when you use it too often, you lose credibility. Always use 'I can do it by...' and if necessary renegotiate the due date. If you can't do it by the due date, you have more credibility in the long run by saying so – even saying no. 'No' is being clear. Saying 'try' is vague and people don't know if you will do it or not.

## MOVE AWAY FROM 'MAYBE'

The word 'maybe' has no power. Saying maybe means that you are either avoiding a decision or avoiding taking an action, and this leads to a sort of paralysis. The next time you hear yourself saying maybe, immediately clarify in your mind what you need to think through now in order to move away from a maybe to either a firm yes or no.

## CHANGE FROM 'IT' TO 'I'

How often do you hear people complain that 'It was because of... that I didn't get ahead'? They blame everyone else and start too many sentences with 'It was...' Change from 'It' to 'I'. Take responsibility for your life and take action to build the life you want. Focus on what you want and not on others.

## ELIMINATE 'IF ONLY'

Too many people use the words 'if only' far too often. They are always looking into the past and wishing things turned out differently. They worry about and want to control the past and the future. All good things come from concentrating our energies and taking action in the present. Eliminate 'if only' from your vocabulary and act in the present.

## ELIMINATE THE WORDS 'I WANT TO STOP...'

We all have things we wish we would stop doing, but a good phrase to eliminate from both our thinking and talking would be "I want to stop..." The reason is that you have to think and focus on the very thing you want to stop in order to tell yourself you want to stop it. It is keeping you focused on what you really don't want to do. A much better way is to replace what you want to stop doing with something you want to do more of. Try it. It works!

Words are, of course, the most powerful drug used by mankind.
*Rudyard Kipling*

FOCUS
ON THE WORDS
YOU USE

AS THEY CAN
GIVE YOU
POWER

## BUY STOCK IN YOURSELF

You buy a certain company's stock because you see the potential in the company to perform, and you invest money in the company. Why not buy stock in yourself? You do that by investing time for your own self-development because you see the potential in you.

## REMINDING OURSELVES OF OUR FULL POTENTIAL

We tend to focus on others and how they could use their full potential more, and often forget to remind ourselves of our own potential. A great definition of success is achieving a worthy goal that utilises our full potential. Remind yourself of your full potential, and you will set goals and take action to make more use of it.

## COMPARE YOURSELF TO YOUR POTENTIAL

True competitors do not really compare themselves to their competition, but to their own potential. Comparing yourself to the competition sets limits on yourself and you will not see the opportunities that are within your potential. From today, compare yourself to your potential.

## PERFORMANCE = POTENTIAL - INTERFERENCE

A great way to look at performance is that it is potential minus interference. We all have potential well beyond what we are currently achieving, and it is the interference (our own limiting beliefs and the circumstances they create) that gets in our way. By changing your beliefs, you begin to create the circumstances for greater performance. You begin using your full potential as the interference just melts away.

## WAKE UP YOUR POTENTIAL

Everyone has enormous potential inside them. Why do some choose to use it and others do not? The ones who use their potential develop a passion and focus that wakes up the potential inside them. What's your passion? Bring a focus to that passion and you will wake up the potential that is inside you.

The potential of the average person is like a huge ocean unsailed, a new continent unexplored, a world of possibilities waiting to be released and channeled toward some great good.

*Brian Tracy*

BUY STOCK
IN YOU

AND YOU DEVELOP
YOUR
POTENTIAL

TIME TO GET
*started*

## HOW DO YOU DEFINE SUCCESS?

One of the least understood things for everyone is how they would define success for themselves. If you don't define it well, then how can you achieve it or even know when you have it? A great thing to do now is to take an hour and create a draft of how you would define success.

## A CLEAR, CONSISTENT FOCUS

Successful people have one thing in common, which is something unsuccessful people lack. That is, a clear, consistent focus. Successful people have clearly determined what it is they want and consider everything else 'off their radar screen'. It is unbelievable what you can accomplish if you keep a clear, consistent focus on what you want.

## ADAPTABILITY – A GREAT QUALITY FOR SUCCESS

There are many qualities that successful people have. However, one key quality is adaptability. Being adaptable means being open to new ideas, and understanding that success doesn't always follow a straight path. What is your level of adaptability?

## YOU CANNOT MEASURE WHAT IS NOT DEFINED

Almost nothing really gets improved unless it is first measured and the performance tracked. However, you can't really measure something unless it has been defined well. Take the time to define the most important outcomes, and then define the measures very well, right from the beginning.

## ALL THE SKILLS OF SUCCESS ARE LEARNABLE

What is interesting is the way unsuccessful people often think that successful people are just lucky. Success really doesn't come from luck. It comes from the discipline the successful people have that enables them to learn all the skills of success. Build the discipline in you to learn those skills too.

Success means having the courage, the determination, and the will to become the person you believe you were meant to be.

*George Sheehan*

## SUCCESS
## IS NOT ABOUT
## LUCK

### IT IS ABOUT THE DETERMINATION TO ACHIEVE IT

## THE GREATEST ILLUSION – I NEED TO BE PUMPED UP

One of the greatest illusions in life is that we need to be pumped up to take action. Successful people don't feel pumped up all the time, but they are always taking action towards their goals. They know that they can't wait to feel pumped up and that inspiration comes only after they take the action. Don't wait to be pumped up, and take action now.

## FEEL THE FEELINGS AND GET STARTED ANYWAY

We all procrastinate with getting started on some tasks because we don't feel like it. However, almost always after we start that task we get the inspiration and energy then to finish it and do it well. It is just getting started that is the difficult thing. Remember, feel the feelings, but get started anyway.

## INCLUDE THE FEELING OF INCOMPETENCE

If you think about it, when you try anything new, you always have a feeling of incompetence at first until you master it. However, many people try to avoid the feeling of incompetence and don't try anything new. You always need to be trying new things in order to stretch yourself and move forward in life. Therefore, include the feeling of incompetence. It's normal, so just take the action and get started.

## YOUR REASONS FOR 'NOT DOING' ARE NOT VALID

Whenever you see yourself procrastinating on something, why not take a look at the reasons why you are delaying action. Those reasons are probably not valid, and by looking at those reasons, it will drive you towards taking the action you have been avoiding.

## DO THE THING YOU FEAR MOST

You may have heard the above saying many times, but have you seen the real power in it? Successful people make a habit of doing what unsuccessful people are afraid to do. They put in place the key habits that will keep them moving in the direction of their goals, and often it is doing the things they fear most that make them successful. An example is in sales or cold-calling. Salespeople fear cold-calling because of hearing 'no' too often, but those who do it anyway begin to improve and eventually to like it. So, to be more successful, do those things you fear most.

Procrastination is giving up what you want most for what you want now.
*Harold Taylor*

DON'T WAIT
FOR THE
INSPIRATION

## DECISIONS ARE THE POWER OF CHANGE

The decisions you make in your life provide the power behind your changes. Think back and you will recall that every major step forward in your life has been launched by taking a decision. What decisions do you need to make in order to launch another major step forward?

## LOOK AT DECISION-MAKING AS A PROCESS

Too many managers look at decision-making as an event rather than a process. To be successful in reaching decisions that stick, you need to think of decision-making as a process, and think through how best to capture the buy-in of the right people upfront. That way you get decisions that stick.

## MAKE DECISIONS EARLY

To accomplish more, it is important to make decisions early and not procrastinate. The most effective leaders always focus their energy on the decision-making process and ensuring that decisions are made at the earliest possible point in the process. You have probably noticed that you have been better off when you made important decisions earlier and didn't procrastinate.

## POWER OF A COMMITTED DECISION

There is nothing more powerful in the world than a committed decision. Many people think they are making decisions, but unless there is a powerful commitment behind those decisions, they are not decisions but preferences. Make sure your decisions are real decisions (not preferences) and add the commitment.

## ACT ON NEW IDEAS QUICKLY

We all get new ideas every day. However, successful people make fast decisions on which ideas are worth pursuing and take action right way on those ideas. Get in the habit of taking action right away on your new ideas.

More than anything else, I believe it's our decisions, not the conditions of our lives, that determine our destiny.

*Anthony Robbins*

# DECISIONS
## ARE THE STARTERS

# THEY ENABLE
# ACTION
## AND PROGRESS

# TIME TO GET *started*

## LIFE IS A NOW MOMENT

It is what you do today and every day that creates your life, and you could say that life is a NOW moment. It is what you are NOW that is either taking you closer to or further away from your goals (i.e. what you want!). Therefore, always think of your life as a NOW moment.

## ARE YOU WILLING TO BE DIFFERENT?

Look at most successful people and all of them have broken away from the masses and tried something different. Often when people do this, they face many challenges early on. Unsuccessful people decide that these challenges are too difficult and stop. Successful people find ways to address the challenges and keep moving forward. Are you willing to be different?

## 'I'D LOVE TO_____, BUT I HATE TO _____.'

Do you ever hear yourself saying the above: 'I'd love to... but I hate to...'? Nothing in life worth achieving is without effort, and we always get out of life what we put into it. The difference is that successful people will do the things they hate to do in order to get the things they love. It's not that successful people like to do everything, they just know they need to do it to get to the goals they have defined. Why? Because they know that doing the necessary now will give them all the time they want for what they like to do in the future. For example: 'I would love to be in good shape, but I hate to exercise.' 'I would love to speak a foreign language, but I hate studying.' Do something you hate in order to get that something you would really love.

## STAY FUTURE-FOCUSED, BUT 'BE PRESENT'

We all need to have goals and be focused on the future, as well as have a picture in our minds of achieving that future. However, it is the action we take in the present that creates the future we want. Be present and take action now (today). If you delay, you are delaying the future you want.

## GET EXCITED ABOUT THE JOURNEY

Goals are extremely important, especially if you want to be successful. However, it is the journey towards those goals that is your life. Why not get as excited about the journey (right now) as you are about your goals?

Go for it now. The future is promised to no one.

*Wayne Dyer*

DISCIPLINE
IS BASED UPON

WHAT YOU DO
NOW
(TODAY)

## MAKE CHANGE SOMETHING NORMAL

People really don't like change. However, our world is changing at such a fast pace that change is now normal. That's a great way to think about it. Change is normal. If you are not changing, then people are moving right past you; in life, in work and to the success you want. So, from today, think 'change is normal' and don't hold back.

## FAILURE TO CHANGE IS FATAL

The biggest failure in life is the failure to change; the world is changing at a faster and faster pace, driven by communications capabilities and new technologies. We all need to change in order to grow and become the person we are capable of being. What is your rate of change, and are you keeping pace with the changing world?

## CHANGE YOURSELF FIRST

Too many people wait for things to change in their outer world (external events) before making a change in their inner world (themselves). They could be waiting forever! If you really want your circumstances to change, you need to change first. Your outer world is a reflection of your inner world. Change yourself and your whole world will change.

## DIFFICULTY = YOUR RESISTANCE TO CHANGE

We all struggle with new things at first and often we don't like change. We think it is too hard, too difficult. However, did you ever realise that we are the ones that are making things difficult? Our level of resistance to change either makes the task easy or difficult. Accept change as a given, and everything will become easier for you.

## STAY AHEAD OF CHANGE

Successful people and companies set themselves up to stay ahead of change. They take the time to think about the future and how they can be even more successful by changing before others see the need to. Invest the time to think ahead and you too will stay ahead of change.

There are two primary choices in life: to accept conditions as they exist, or accept the responsibility for changing them.

*Denis Waitley*

CHANGE
IS ALL AROUND US

BE THE ONE IN
FRONT
OF THE CHANGE

## HAPPINESS – DECIDE ON AHEAD OF TIME

Being happy is never down to what others do for us, or from our environment. Others cannot make us happy, as our happiness has to come from within us (it's our choice). A good way to look at it is that happiness is something you decide on ahead of time (it is not dependent on others).

## BEING HAPPY – IT'S JUST A DECISION

Too often people say that they will be happy 'when' or 'if' something happens. They are waiting for external changes before they make an internal decision. You have it within yourself to be happy. It's just a decision for you to make. So, don't wait for the 'when' or 'if' and make the decision to be happy today.

## DOING BETTER THAN GOOD

If you want to keep a positive attitude through the day, and also make an impact on the people you meet, why not say, 'I'm doing better than good!' You have heard the quote 'our thoughts make us' – so we should use our language to help keep us positive and to influence others. Why not be 'better than good' today, tomorrow and every day?

## KEEPING YOUR SENSE OF HUMOUR

As we go through life, we are always going to face problems along the way, both big and small. Keeping our sense of humour and the ability to have fun along the way not only makes life more enjoyable, but also helps to prevent us from becoming too stressed out. There's a wonderful old quote that says: "A person without a sense of humour is like a wagon without springs. It's jolted by every pebble on the road" – Henry Ward Beecher. So, why not go through today with a smile on your face and look at the funny side of life?

## HAPPINESS BEGINS WHEN SELFISHNESS ENDS

True happiness begins when we become less selfish and more caring of others. People grow long-term in the support or service of others and never at the expense of others. Set a goal to help others and you will receive back in other ways many times your efforts.

Happiness is not something ready made. It comes from your own actions.

*Dalai Lama*

HAPPINESS
IS NOT SOMETHING
THAT HAPPENS
TO US

WE MAKE IT
HAPPEN
FOR OURSELVES
AND OTHERS

# TIME TO GET *started*

## WANT TO BE MORE CREATIVE? TALK TO CREATIVE PEOPLE

If you want to be more creative in your thoughts, one good way is to talk to more creative people. Many of you have heard the initials OPM (Other People's Money). Why not use OPI (Other People's Ideas) to trigger more ideas and more creativity in yourself? Pick a few creative friends or co-workers and spend time talking with them.

## HOW DO YOU FEED YOUR CREATIVITY?

Everyone has their own special times when they are most creative, and there are often different ways that everyone's creativity gets triggered. However, we all need to also feed our creativity by the books we read, the CDs we listen to, and the experiences from the people we meet each week. What are the best ways you feed your creativity?

## TO INCREASE YOUR CREATIVITY, DO A LITTLE MIND MAPPING...

There is a saying that in order to get a great idea, get lots of ideas. One really good way to get lots of ideas is to mind map. It helps to get all the ideas out of your head. Its free-form approach makes sure that you are not limited by any sequential thinking that making a list creates. Doing mind maps often can also help to boost your creativity.

## IDEAS AND ACTION – TWO MAIN INGREDIENTS FOR SUCCESS

If you think about it, two of the main ingredients for success are ideas and action. It is the quality of your ideas that drives the quality in your actions. Keep this in mind and do a little more upfront thinking to make sure that you are generating the best ideas you can. Then, take action on them right away.

## IDEA TIME – WHAT'S YOURS?

Getting new ideas is how we improve things. More importantly, it is how we keep our energy at a high level. How, where and when do you get your best ideas? Put yourself in that situation more often and see your ideas soar, as well as your energy.

You can't use up creativity. The more you use, the more you have.

*Maya Angelou*

# CREATIVITY IS WITHIN ALL OF US

## AND WE JUST NEED TO DEVELOP THE TRIGGER

## OUR THOUGHTS ARE OUR CURRENCY

A really great way to look at the power of our thoughts is to think of them as currency. We can accomplish whatever we turn our thoughts to. If we invest our time thinking, then we get a return. If we spend out time in other ways (TV, etc.), we get hardly any return. Remember, our thoughts are our currency.

## INCREASE YOUR THINKING TIME

Today's life moves at such a fast pace that we sometimes don't stop long enough to get in some quality thinking time. However, it is our thinking time that produces ideas and possible actions that help us make step changes in our lives and how we do things. If you feel you are not improving at the rate you would like, maybe you should increase your thinking time.

## WHAT IS YOUR DOMINANT THOUGHT?

They say you are what you think about. So, if that is true, what is your dominant thought each day? To be successful in life, your dominant thought should be on your most important goals. Successful people's dominant thoughts are always on their most important goals (and not on anything else).

## THE MORE YOU THINK, THE LESS THE STRUGGLE

Take any area in your life that is a struggle right now. Chances are that you have been avoiding thinking about that area and it is not getting any better, or even getting worse. You are avoiding the very thing that will help. The more thinking time you apply to that area, the more ideas will come to you on how to make things better.

## YOU ARE WHAT YOU THINK

You are the person you are today because of the way that you have thought in the past. Many people blame others or say it was because of 'him' or 'her' that I didn't advance. It is never because of 'them'; it's because of 'us' and how we thought. Your thinking can change and you can change. Think in possibilities and anything is possible.

The life you are leading is simply a reflection of your thinking.

*Doug Firebaugh*

WHEN WE BEGIN
THINKING
WE CAN BEGIN
CHANGING

## FAILURE IS PART OF THE PROCESS OF SUCCESS

Successful people have experienced some type of failure during their life. For them, failure was just part of the process towards their success. Yes, they took a step backwards, but they learned from what happened and then took action to move forward again. Failure is never final. Treat it as another lesson and get back into action quickly.

## YOU MAKE MISTAKES – MISTAKES DO NOT MAKE YOU

Often when we make a mistake we personalise it too much. We believe we are a mistake (or a failure). When successful people make a mistake, they review why they made the mistake, understand the learning, and then move on right away. You can too. Everyone makes mistakes. Just remember to learn from them and leave it there.

## THE DOER MAKES MISTAKES

You could say that the person who reaches his or her goals the fastest is the one who makes the most mistakes. Successful people know this best. They take action and if it doesn't work, they try something different. Remember, the doer makes mistakes, but also makes things happen.

## IT'S FEEDBACK, NOT FAILURE

There never is a failure in your life unless you don't learn from the experience. Failure, when you take the learnings, is really feedback. It is highlighting a way that doesn't work and gives you learnings and insights to do better the next time.

## PEOPLE DON'T FAIL, THEY JUST QUIT

Failure is often a matter of quitting. We try a few ways that don't work out the way we want and then just quit. Successful people know that they will need to adapt their approach in order to reach their goals. They have determined that they will not quit until they reach their goals, and keep at it until they find the right way there.

Mistakes are part of the dues one pays for a full life.
*Sophia Loren*

FAILURE
IS NEVER
PERMANENT

ONLY FEEDBACK
TO START
AGAIN IN A
BETTER WAY

## TAKE AWAY YOUR LEARNING – THEN FOCUS ON THE FUTURE

Often people dwell on the past too much. They play over and over again (like a stuck record) the mistakes they have made. Every time they do this, they reinforce in their mind those mistakes. With the past, we should only bring back a memory in order to learn from it. Once we have the learning (understanding how to do it better the next time), we need to look forward. So the next time you feel yourself focusing on the past, just look for the learning, and move on to focus on the present and the actions that will drive you towards a different and brighter future.

## DON'T LET PAST EXPERIENCES STOP YOU

You are not your past. In fact, you are what you think, and you can change the thinking of the past to a thinking of the future. It is just up to you to take the decision to do it. Change your thinking and you can change your life. Just decide today.

## TURN OFF THE REPLAY BUTTON

Most people spend too much time thinking about the past and not concentrating their focus and energy on what they can do right now and into the future. It is like they are constantly pressing the replay button. Why not turn the replay button off and focus on what you can do, rather than what you would have done differently?

## THE SELF-SABOTAGE PRINCIPLE

One of the most dangerous obstacles we put in our own way is the idea that we don't deserve success, and base this on our past. We often evaluate our own abilities in a negative way, and when opportunities come our way, we act as if we are not good enough to take advantage of them. Don't self-sabotage your success; believe in your own abilities.

## YOUR PAST DOES NOT EQUAL YOUR FUTURE

There are too many people who have the equation in their head that their past equals their future. That is only true if they don't change the way they are thinking. However, we all have the ability to change our thinking, and the day we do is the first day of our completely new future.

Your past is not your potential. In any hour you can choose to liberate the future.

*Marilyn Ferguson*

## INTEGRITY – THE QUALITY THAT GUARANTEES ALL THE OTHERS

Integrity is the most important quality to have. Integrity is the visible way that others can feel confident that you will live up to the rest of your values. Without integrity, other people might have a question on everything you do. Protect your integrity. People will then have more confidence in you, and you will see more people willing to help you along the way.

## BE HONEST WITH YOURSELF

The person you need to be the most honest with is yourself. If you are honest in your evaluation of your strengths and weaknesses, you will drive a much more focused personal development plan. Just keep in mind that an honest appraisal of your talents will focus your growth in areas where you will get the biggest return.

## BE CAREFUL OF GOALS/VALUES CONFLICT

One of the biggest problems people experience at times is the conflict between their goals and their values. For you to truly commit to your goals, you need to make sure that your behaviours are consistent with your values. If they are not consistent, your actions will prevent you from reaching your goals. If they are consistent, your values will become a powerful enabler.

## A WISHBONE WITHOUT A BACKBONE IS USELESS

Many people wish for a better life, but lack the discipline and focus to take the sustained action to make it happen. It is good to dream and visualise what you want in life, but you have to follow that up with the action as well. A wishbone without a backbone is useless.

## BE TRUE TO YOURSELF

The one thing that everyone wants to do is to live with integrity. That means that we need to be true to ourselves and really know who we are. Who we are is based upon the principles we choose to live by, and the habits and behaviours we show to others and ourselves. Be true to yourself.

Real integrity is doing the right thing, knowing that nobody's going to know whether you did it or not.

*Oprah Winfrey*

INTEGRITY
IS LIKE A DAM

WE MUST
ALWAYS
BE ADDRESSING
ANY CRACKS

## BE PROACTIVE VS. REACTIVE

The world is moving at such a fast pace these days. People are not really taking the time to think, and end up spending their entire week in a very reactive way. They are constantly being influenced by events and other people. Take the time to think ahead and be proactive in the way you set the focus for your next week. This allows you to take consistent action towards your focus and not let people divert you to other things.

## TENTATIVE IS AN EXPRESSION OF WEAKNESS

If you really want something in life, you have to be active and go get it. Your own self-esteem, confidence and strength come from the very actions you take. When you are tentative, you are really expressing your weakness.

## BEING 'TENTATIVE' HAS NO POWER

How many times do we take a 'tentative' approach to something? Being tentative comes from a position of weakness and not from a position of power. Move away from being tentative and take action towards what you want. Action creates inspiration and inspiration creates power.

## IF YOU HALF-PLAY, YOU LOSE

Anything done halfway is never successful. With anything in life, if you don't give it 100%, you lose. We often take on too many things and end up playing at 50% on everything. Pick a few key things in your life and play at 100% on them for the next month, and you will see the difference.

## BE A 'GO TO' PERSON

One of the best compliments you could ever get is that others view you as a 'Go To' person. That means that you have the attitude and determination always to deliver on what you set out to do. Would your co-workers and friends describe you as a 'Go To' person?

The most important key to achieving great success is to decide upon your goal and launch, get started, take action, move.

*John Wooden*

ACTIVE
IS THE ENEMY OF
PASSIVE

AS NOTHING GETS
ACCOMPLISHED
WITHOUT
ACTION

## SELF-ESTEEM IS YOUR REPUTATION WITH YOURSELF

A great way to look at self-esteem is that it is your reputation with yourself. If you have a good reputation with others, it means that they have confidence in you, your character and your abilities. The same can apply to you. When you have high self-esteem you have the confidence in your character and abilities to create the success you desire. How is your reputation with yourself?

## MANAGE YOUR BRAND (YOUR REPUTATION)

Just like companies, we as individuals have an image we project to others, and it is our brand. Our brand (or reputation) is based on the way we behave with respect to our relationships and the way we keep our commitments. Manage yourself as a brand and your reputation will soar.

## IMAGINE YOURSELF LIVING IT

The people who build a successful life for themselves imagine living it first. The action of imagining themselves living it creates passion inside them that they now need it, and this builds the 'Why' behind having it. Build your 'Why' by imagining the successful life you want, and you will build the passion and drive to go and get it.

## CLEAN UP YOUR SELF-IMAGE

Many people are held back from achieving what they are capable of by their self-image. What they are really saying to themselves is, 'I am my past.' Being stuck in the past means that they will continue to get what they had in the past. Let go of the past and think in possibilities, and you will then create a self-image based on the future. Continually focusing on possibilities will pull your self-image, and you, to the future you really want.

## WHEN YOU GET THERE, ACT LIKE YOU BELONG

Our beliefs are sometimes the only thing that stands in our way. We don't go after bigger challenges because 'inside' we think we are not good enough. Start thinking from today that you can do it, and when you get there, act like you belong.

Our self-image, strongly held, essentially determines what we become.

*Maxwell Maltz*

YOUR SELF-IMAGE
IS LIKE A
BLUEPRINT
FOR YOUR LIFE

CREATE IT TO BE
AS POSITIVE
AND CLEAR AS
POSSIBLE

## PERSISTENCE – SURRENDERING TO YOUR PURPOSE

A good definition of persistence is 'surrendering to your purpose'. When you have a strong purpose (goal), persistence is merely accepting to do all that is necessary to achieve it. Surrender to your purpose today and you can achieve the life you want faster than you think.

## THE 'WILL' TO WIN CREATES THE 'WAY' TO WIN

It is often the 'Will' that creates the 'Way'. People with the 'Will' to win do whatever is necessary to reach the goals they define. That 'Will' is contagious and they also attract the help of others who want to help them with the 'Way'. Build your will to win and that will create the way to win.

## POWER OF SUSTAINED EFFORT

Some people think that to become successful you need some type of magic or luck (or even to be super-intelligent). However, the difference is that successful people put in sustained effort. Day in and day out, they do all that's necessary for them to reach their goals. Keep up a sustained effort from now on.

## THERE'S NEVER A STRAIGHT LINE TO YOUR GOALS

In whatever you do in life, there is never a perfect path (straight line) to your goals. There are always some adjustments you will need to make, and it is the adjustments that help you to grow. Expect the adjustments (they are normal), and stay focused on your goals.

## BE A FINISHER IN A WORLD OF STARTERS

Ask any successful person and almost all would say that they became successful because they did not quit. The world is full of starters who stop when the going gets tough. People who start something and stick with it are the ones who achieve success. Be a finisher and achieve the success you deserve.

Persistence makes up for a lack of capital and an abundance of mistakes while it levels the playing field like no other virtue.

*Vic Johnson*

## PERSISTENCE WILL DELIVER SUCCESS TO YOU

## WHILE OTHERS QUIT AND GIVE UP

## YOU ARE WHAT YOU SETTLED FOR

Your life is the way it is now, based on all the things you settled for over the years. Basically, you arrived to where you are now based on the choices you have made. For a better life, you need to make better choices, and that means never settling for something if you know it's not helping you to become all you can be. What have you settled for recently?

## MAKING THE RIGHT CHOICES

If you think about it, our lives are all about making choices. To make choices, we always need some type of criteria. For our lives, the goals we set and review frequently provide the criteria for the choices that we make and what we choose to do and not to do. Remember, goals help us to make the right choices.

## DON'T MAJOR IN MINOR THINGS

Very often we all fall into the trap of being diverted to small tasks that are not moving us closer to our goals. We might feel better because we think we are accomplishing a great deal, but are we? Unless we are focused on activities that will help us reach our goals, we are majoring in minor things. Therefore, watch what you focus on. Why not major in major things today?

## THE CHOICES YOU MAKE, MAKE YOU

When you think about it, the choices you make in life determine the life you will have. Most people don't really spend the time to think through those choices well enough before making them. Remember: the better your thinking, the better your choices, and the better the life you will create.

## IMPORTANT ENOUGH TO MAKE TIME

We all say it: 'If I had more time I would like to...' The reason we haven't done it is because we haven't made it important enough to make time for it. Review each week what is important to you, and you will make time for what you have made important.

It is our choices... that show what we truly are, far more than our abilities.

*J. K. Rowling*

YOU MAKE YOUR
LIFE'S
CHOICES

AND THEN YOUR
CHOICES
MAKE YOU

## LIFE-LONG LEARNING

It is good to think about your own development as life-long learning. Our learning and development never stop, and we should always be on the lookout for new ideas. Set your learning goals just as you would set any other goals in your life.

## WHAT DO I NEED TO LEARN?

If we have ambitious goals, it will always push us to grow and become more than we are today. A good question to ask ourselves each week is, 'What do I need to learn?', and then take some action to learn it. The limiting factor for your future success is the speed at which you grow yourself.

## BECOME A 'SPONGE'

Take in every new experience you can. Read as much as you can. Every experience you have and everything you read is building a stronger foundation for yourself. Being like a 'sponge' and soaking up all the experiences and learning will make you more valuable to your employer and to your customers. Better yet, become a sort of a 'super-sponge' in what you are best at, and become the expert in your field. You will be amazed at how valuable your learning time will become as your time investment will yield an unbelievable payoff.

## LEARN FROM THE EXPERTS

Too often we struggle with something and are afraid to ask for help from others. You know, we can never advance in life by trying to learn everything on our own and in our own time. There are not enough hours in the day! The people who advance quickly are those who continually learn from experts or mentors, and apply what they have learned immediately. Is there someone who could be a good mentor for you? Learn from the experts and grow faster.

## LEARN AND APPLY

A great little phrase to remember is to 'learn and apply'. We are learning something new every day. However, what we learn stays with us longer when we apply it very soon after the learning. Whatever you learn today and this week, look to apply it as soon as you can.

The only true security in life comes from knowing that every single day you are improving yourself in some way.

*Anthony Robbins*

## LEARNING NEEDS TO BE A HABIT

### AND A DAILY ONE TO CREATE THE SUCCESS YOU DESIRE

## WHAT ARE YOUR PERSONAL GROWTH GOALS?

We get more out of life and more opportunities when we develop ourselves to do more. However, most people haven't set goals for their development and without goals they develop at a much slower pace. Why? Their development has no focus. Give your personal development a focus and establish your personal growth goals for the next 12 months.

## GROWTH COMES FROM DISCOMFORT

Personal growth comes from taking ourselves out of our comfort zones and stretching ourselves to try new things. Our initial reaction is to stay in our comfort zone, but that really means not growing. Learn to live outside your comfort zone and you will never stop growing.

## IMPROVE YOURSELF VS. COMPARE YOURSELF

Some people spend more time comparing themselves to others than improving themselves. Simple comparisons to others have no real advantages to you unless you are trying to model the successful behaviours of others to improve your own. Stay away from simple comparisons and concentrate on improving yourself.

## EVALUATED EXPERIENCE IS THE BEST TEACHER

They say that experience is the best teacher. However, it is really evaluated experience that is the best teacher. Unless you spend the time to capture the key learnings from your experiences, you don't get to see the change in behaviours you need as clearly as you should.

## WORK HARDER ON YOURSELF

Jim Rohn says, 'Learn to work harder on yourself than you do on your job. Work harder on your job, and you'll make a living. Work harder on yourself, and you can make a fortune.' How true this is! When we work on ourselves, we develop new skills and abilities that enable us to do more than just our present job. As we learn more, we get more excited and want to use these new abilities in more and different ways. So, why not think today – how can I work harder on developing myself, and create an action plan to make it happen?

Change is inevitable, growth is intentional.
*Glenda Cloud*

DEVELOP YOUR
OWN PLANS
AND ACTIONS
TO GROW

NO ONE
CAN GROW
FOR YOU!

TIME TO GET
started

## WE ONLY ACHIEVE TO THE LIMITS OF OUR THOUGHTS

Have you ever noticed that all successful people saw their success in their minds before it happened? They had no limits on their thinking and could think big thoughts. What is your level of thinking today? If you want a better life, remove the limits to your thinking and you can make it happen.

## DON'T REPLAY YOUR LIMITATIONS

There is one thing that, if we could eliminate it, would be a powerful impact on our lives. That is, eliminating the replaying of our limitations. We constantly say to ourselves, 'I can't do that,' or, 'I'm not good at that,' and are really defeated before we even try. Also, we are so clever as to bring up past experiences in our minds that prove we can't do it. Eliminate replaying your limitations and you will be amazed at what you can do.

## LET GO OF YOUR LIMITING THOUGHTS

Many people are really 'boxing themselves in' because of their own limiting thoughts. They see themselves in a way that limits them. See yourself as capable of doing only so much, and you will do 'only so much'. Break free of your limiting thoughts and the sky is the limit.

## RAISE YOUR LEVEL OF THINKING

If you want to raise your level of income, you need to raise your level of thinking. People achieve only to the limits of their thinking. When people expand their thinking, they begin to take actions that are consistent with that expanded thinking and accomplish a great deal more and earn more. Raise your level of thinking today.

## ACT AS IF YOU HAVE NO LIMITS

Too many people put limits on the expectations of themselves. In fact, they are their own biggest barriers to achieving what they really want. How about you? Do you put your own limits on what you can do? In reality, there are no limits; only the ones you create for yourself. Therefore, why not act as if you have no limits – today and every day?

The only limitation in your life is the limitation of your own thinking.

*James A. Ray*

THE ONLY REAL
LIMITS
WE HAVE

ARE THE ONES
WE SET FOR
OURSELVES

## TIME MANAGEMENT IS REALLY FOCUS MANAGEMENT

Everyone talks about time management, but you really can't manage time. We are all given the same amount of time, and it is up to us what we do with it. We can only really manage our focus. It is what we focus on, driven by our goals and our discipline to achieve them, that helps us to make the best use of our time. Therefore, we shouldn't think only about saving time on our activities, but what activities we want to do to begin with (that's our focus).

## A SPECIFIC FOCUS WILL TAKE YOU FURTHER

Every successful person will tell you that their success began the instant they believed in themselves and focused all their energy on what they wanted. When you are specific about what you want, you will make the right choices on how you use your time to get it faster. A specific focus will take you further and faster.

## FOCUSED PEOPLE HAVE FEWER THOUGHTS

It sounds a little crazy, but very focused and successful people really have fewer thoughts each day. They know what they want and focus all their thoughts on achieving it. They don't let their mind wander off, thinking about all kinds of other things. Thus, they have fewer thoughts, but the thoughts they have are highly focused on what they want to accomplish. How focused are your thoughts?

## WHAT YOU DON'T NEED TO KNOW

One of the keys to being more focused and productive is to eliminate distractions, and one of the biggest distractions is all the information that is available to us today. You can't know everything, so it is important to focus on information that will help you to reach your goals. Decide what you need to know and what you don't need to know.

## A CLEAR FOCUS CAN KEEP AWAY DISTRACTIONS

In today's world we have so many options for how we use our time. A clear focus on what we want and need to do is very powerful. This power comes from the ability to eliminate the distractions that are not within our focus; in essence, empowering us to say 'no' and keep our focus on what is most important in order to reach our goals.

The three greatest predictors of success that we know of today are focus, passion, and mental toughness.

*Dave Cook*

SUCCESS
ALWAYS STARTS
FROM THE SAME
PLACE
FROM YOUR
FOCUS

## TIME TO GET started

## YOU DON'T GET PAID FOR TIME

In life, your ultimate pay cheque is not based on the time you work, but on the value you provide. Those who just 'put in the time' do not advance and get the rewards from their time. Successful people focus on creating value and making the most of every minute of time.

## ALWAYS LOOK FOR THE DOUBLE AND TRIPLE WINS

Today, we all have so much to do and we need to try to get the most out of each activity and our time. Always look for activities that will give you benefits in multiple areas. An example is exercising while listening to an audio book. You get the physical benefits of the exercise, and also the learning benefits from listening to the audio book. Remember, you get more out of your day when you continually look for these double and even triple wins.

## PROTECT AND VALUE YOUR TIME

Everyone gets the same amount of time in their life, yet some people achieve more with that time than others. They place a high value on their time and protect it for their most important goals in their life. What value do you place on your time? Value your time and you will begin to say 'no' to the good, so that you can say 'yes' to the best.

## WHO DO YOU INVEST TIME WITH?

There is an old saying that you become what you are around. If that's true, how you grow and what you become is greatly influenced by those people you invest your time with. Are the people you invest your time with helping you to grow?

## TRADING TIME AND MONEY

Have you ever noticed how we trade time and money? Early in our careers we trade time for money. We work long hours to make as much money as we can (because we started with nothing). As we get older, we trade money for more time. We buy devices or the help of others to make our life easier in order to use our time in different ways. A good question to ask ourselves: Are we trading time and money in the most effective way?

You may delay, but time will not.

*Benjamin Franklin*

BE ALL AND
ACCOMPLISH
ALL THAT'S POSSIBLE

INVEST
YOUR TIME
WISELY

## MAKE COMMON SENSE A COMMON PRACTICE

You often hear others say something that really is common sense. However, when you think about it, you don't do it for yourself. The successful people make common sense a common practice. They make habits where unsuccessful people do not have the discipline to turn common sense into habits. For your success, make common sense a common practice (a habit).

## TAKE A LOOK AT YOUR HABITS

Just read this excellent quote on habits: 'Chains of habit are too light to be felt until they are too heavy to be broken' from Warren Buffett. Many of us have habits that are not moving us towards our goals, and we haven't woken up to this fact yet. We should all be reviewing our key habits. Are they helping us to achieve our goals or not? If certain habits aren't helping us or are even working against us, then make a plan to change those habits today. Why not do your habits review this week?

## DO WHAT'S NECESSARY

Most of the people won't do things they don't like to do, even if they are really necessary to get ahead in life. The successful people just get on with it and do what is necessary (even if it's something they don't like to do). Since most of the people won't do what is necessary, then there's little competition for you. Do what's necessary today.

## DON'T BREAK A HABIT, REPLACE IT

Habits are hard to create, and even harder to break. When trying to change your behaviour (your habits), try focusing on replacing them with new habits instead of breaking old ones. It is a much more positive approach to replace a bad habit than to try to eliminate it, which is a negative approach. Try replacing habits from now on.

## FOLLOW THE TRACKS OF SUCCESSFUL PEOPLE

If you do (habits and behaviours) as other successful people, you will get the same results. It's really based on the law of cause and effect. Therefore, a good strategy to focus on is to follow the tracks of successful people. Find out what they are doing and put those habits and behaviours into your days and weeks.

We first make our habits,
then our habits make us.
*John Dryden*

# KEY HABITS
## ARE OFTEN EASY TO
# DEFINE

**BUT DIFFICULT
TO MAINTAIN
BE THE ONE
WHO CAN**

## TAKE COMMAND OF YOUR EMOTIONS BY TALKING TO THEM

Whenever people get down and depressed, it is usually because they are listening to their own negative thoughts and building problems up to be larger than they really are. Change from listening to talking to yourself. Say to yourself that, 'Yes, I have this problem, but let's begin thinking what I can do about it.' Begin talking as opposed to listening.

## MOST FATIGUE IS RELATED TO OUR EMOTIONS

Most of the fatigue in our lives is related to our emotions and not something physical. Our physical capabilities are well beyond whatever we normally use, which means our emotions have a tremendous power over our feeling of fatigue. Don't let your emotions trick you into a feeling of fatigue. Do some activity anyway, and you will act your way out of that feeling of fatigue.

## MAKE THE EMOTIONAL LINK

Many times we try to influence or convince someone with logic only. Have you ever noticed that much of the advertising for consumer products doesn't focus on the logic (or the detailed benefits), but on the emotion you will feel if you use their product? Use the same idea when you are trying to influence or convince others. Try to make the emotional link with them.

## WHY DO YOU FEEL THAT WAY?

Whenever one of your employees is behaving in a negative way, a good question to ask is: 'Why do you feel that way?' Often managers ask the employee: 'Why did you do that?', but this is a much more confrontational way to ask them. Sometimes, the question you ask can make a big difference.

## YOU'VE GOT TO FANTASISE TO GET WHAT YOU WANT

If we only look at things in a conservative way, there would not be nearly as many inventions created every day. We all need to fantasise, especially on what we want in life. When we fantasise we engage our emotions and begin to see possibilities that we never knew could be achievable. Fantasise to get what you want, and you will see the possibilities and ideas to action them.

Our emotions need to be as educated as our intellect. It is important to know how to feel, how to respond, and how to let life in so that it can touch you.

*Jim Rohn*

# FEEL THE EMOTIONS

# AND TAKE THE ACTION ANYWAY

## COMMIT YOURSELF

Commitment is what turns a dream into reality. Until you truly commit yourself to something, that something stays more like a dream. Commitment drives the need for a plan to get there and the discipline to execute what's on the plan. Commit yourself and your dream will become a reality.

## HOW MUCH OF YOU IS IN THE GAME?

A great question to ask yourself is, 'How much of me is in the game?' Too often we go through life just going through the motions, without really being engaged in what we are doing. Basically, you get out of life what you put into it. The more of you there is in the game of life, the more the game goes your way.

## REGARDLESS OF... YOU MAKE IT HAPPEN

When we have big goals, we will always have challenges that will get in our way. A good phrase to keep in our heads is that 'regardless of...' any challenges that come our way, we will always find a way to succeed. People who say 'because of...' usually make excuses, versus the people who say 'regardless of...' and always make it happen.

## KEEP YOUR COMMITMENTS

If you want to be successful and feel good about it, learn to keep your commitments (both to others and especially to yourself). When you honour your commitments, you build the discipline and confidence that provides the fuel for greater achievement. Skip a few commitments and it's like your fuel tank has a slow leak. Honour your commitments to keep your fuel tank full, and achieve everything you can.

## COMMITMENT TRANSFORMS A PROMISE INTO REALITY

You have heard about commitment and how important it is. One of the best ways to describe commitment is turning a promise made to yourself and/or others into reality. It is commitment that makes 'real' what we want in life.

A commitment is like your signature on a contract: it binds you to a course of action.

*Nido Qubein*

COMMITMENT
AND OWNERSHIP
GO HAND
IN HAND

AND WITH THEM
ANYTHING
IS POSSIBLE

## ACTION PRECEDES MOTIVATION

Too many people wait to feel motivated to take action. It really doesn't work that way; action precedes motivation. Picture a snowball going down a hill. It is picking up snow (more motivation) as it goes down the hill, and it becomes bigger and stronger. However, that snowball wouldn't have existed at all unless someone had made it first and then started it rolling. Like the snowball, if we make the action, we'll get the motivation, which will get bigger and stronger. Take action today!

## ENOUGH MOTIVATION TO GET STARTED

People are always looking for the motivation to do what is necessary to get what they want in life. To take the action on what we need to do, just learn to develop enough motivation to get started. Most of us get the inspiration to finish the action once we get started on it. Build the motivation inside to just get started, and you will accomplish more in life.

## CREATE YOUR OWN SOURCES OF MOTIVATION

Too many people expect others to motivate them. It really doesn't work that way and we need continually to find our own sources of motivation. Remember: people who are self-motivated will always be the leaders of those who are not.

## THINK BACK TO A SUCCESSFUL TIME

A powerful visualising exercise used by athletes is to think back in time and replay an occasion when they were really successful. Bringing back the memories of past successes brings confidence to them today. You can use these same visualising techniques that athletes do. Think back to a successful time and watch how it brings you more confidence right now, in whatever you are doing.

## LISTEN TO MOTIVATIONAL CDs TO KEEP YOUR THOUGHTS POSITIVE

Everyone feels down from time to time. However, if you are constantly feeding yourself positive thoughts, there will be no room in your head for the negative ones. Take the opportunity to listen to motivational CDs often. Fill your mind with the possibilities and soon nothing will seem impossible.

People often say that motivation doesn't last. Well, neither does bathing... that's why we recommend it daily.
*Zig Ziglar*

FEED YOUR
MOTIVATION
DAILY

IT WILL KEEP
YOUR ENERGY
HIGH

## YOU CAN'T SEE THE PICTURE WHEN YOU'RE IN THE FRAME

Many people get so consumed in their day-to-day problems that they don't see the opportunities that are really right in front of them. They need to step back from the day-to-day and look at things in a broader perspective to see those opportunities. Remember, you can't see the full picture (the opportunities) when you are in the frame.

## PICTURE IT IN YOUR MIND

Your world starts by what you are thinking and picturing in your mind. Your thinking is like the fuel that drives the engine of your life. Therefore, the quality of your life is in direct proportion to the quality of your thinking and what you are picturing your life to be. Why not set a little time aside each day to do more quality thinking and picturing the life you really want?

## SEE IT COMPLETED AND IN PLACE

If you want to be more successful in life, you need to see your goals completed and everything in place. The power behind the actions to achieve your goals always comes from how well you picture them. Picture your goals completed and in as many details as possible, and you will add real power to your actions.

## SEE IT AND BELIEVE IT

See it and you've got direction. Believe it and you'll get there. People have learned that you need to see it (visualise it) in order to get it. You need to see yourself achieving those goals. However, that's not enough and many people stop there. You also need to believe it as well. You need to have 100% belief in yourself to make it happen. See and believe – then make it happen.

## DON'T WORK AT HALF POWER (USE YOUR SUBCONSCIOUS MIND)

Visualising what you want is like making a 'mental blueprint' of your goals, and provides your subconscious mind with plans to work on. It is the same as dreaming about a certain new car and suddenly you see them everywhere. You gave your subconscious mind a 'mental blueprint' of what you wanted. So, don't work at half power – give your subconscious mind the 'mental blueprint' to work on.

How different our lives are when we really know what is deeply important to us, and keeping that picture in mind, we manage ourselves each day to be and to do what really matters most.

*Stephen Covey*

WHAT WE
PICTURE
WE CAN
ACCOMPLISH

## TRANSFORM DIFFERENCES INTO OPPORTUNITIES

You can see this as a real opportunity if you have a diverse team of individuals. Use their differences to generate more creativity in your discussions. Too many managers do just the opposite by trying to introduce processes, etc. that aim to make everyone think in the same way. Always look to transform differences into opportunities.

## MAGNIFY YOUR BLESSINGS AS MUCH AS YOUR DISAPPOINTMENTS

We all tend to exaggerate our disappointments and spend little time thinking about our blessings. This creates an image of our lives being much worse than they really are. Magnify your blessings and you will have a much more balanced and positive image of your life.

## DON'T SUFFER FROM POSSIBILITY-BLINDNESS

Some people wouldn't see a possibility if it was staring them in the face. They have possibility-blindness. These people have such a negative attitude and mindset that the possibilities and opportunities that come their way are never seen. Remember, a positive attitude prevents possibility-blindness, and suddenly you see opportunities everywhere.

## BE A REALISTIC OPTIMIST

You often hear motivational speakers talk about being positive and optimistic. Being positive is the place to start, but taking action on those positive thoughts is going to make you successful. If you don't take action, your optimism is not based on anything real. Be a realistic optimist and take the action.

## THE HARDER YOU WORK, THE MORE LUCK YOU HAVE

Hard work produces luck. We have all heard this, but have we really understood why? Hard work means that we have done the thinking and preparation. Therefore, when luck (the opportunity) comes our way, we are in the position to take advantage of it. Are you in the position to take advantage of luck (opportunities) today?

Opportunities are usually disguised as hard work, so most people don't recognize them.

*Ann Landers*

TAKE
ACTION
AND YOU WILL
ATTRACT
OPPORTUNITIES

## OUTCOME THINKING OPENS UP MORE POSSIBILITIES

People who think in outcomes come up with more creative ways to accomplish what they want. In essence, it opens up more possibilities. When you are clear on your outcomes, you always see more ways to reach those outcomes, and you can choose the ways that get you there the fastest (in the least activities). Remember, outcome thinking opens up more possibilities.

## BUILD YOUR DAYS AROUND YOUR HIGHEST PRIORITIES

Too many people let their days fill up with activities that are not connected with the highest priorities. They don't think ahead and plan their days, so others steal time from them and often before they even notice it. Remember: build your days in advance (think ahead) with activities connected with your highest priorities.

## YOU HAVE TO HAVE THOUGHT BEFORE

In order to be more productive during the day, you can't always be thinking, 'What do I do next?' That slows you down. You need to think about your day (and your week) before it hits you. Take a little time at the end of each day and think about what needs to be accomplished the next day. Also, take an hour each week to think about what you need to accomplish in the coming week. A little upfront thinking goes a long way to make the best use of your time.

## NEVER WITH THE SAME THOUGHT TWICE

Productive people always have something to write with wherever they go. They want to capture and write down the ideas that come to them so that they can make good use of them later. They have a motto: 'Never with the same thought twice.' Capture your ideas down on paper today.

## WHAT GETS TRACKED GETS DONE

There is an old saying that what gets measured gets done. It is also true that what gets tracked gets done, especially in the follow-up of commitments made to you by others. It is useful to keep a follow-up list, and keep track of what others have committed to do for you and by when. When you track and follow up other people's commitments to you, they take action.

Productivity is never an accident. It is always the result of a commitment to excellence, intelligent planning, and focused effort.

*Paul J. Meyer*

WHEN YOU
PLAN

PRODUCTIVITY
FOLLOWS

## DON'T LET PEOPLE TALK YOU OUT OF IT

When we try new things in life we will always find people telling us that it can't be done. Too often we let people talk us out of something because our picture of what we want is not strong enough in our minds. Also, too many people try to pull us down in order to lift themselves up. Be strong in what you want and don't let others talk you out of it.

## DON'T LET OTHERS STEAL YOUR DREAMS

There are a number of people in the world who are dissatisfied with their lives and are always putting down others who are trying to make their life better. If you meet people like this, don't let them steal your dreams. Anything is possible if you have the desire and the will to discipline yourself to do what's necessary to go get it.

## DON'T BUY INTO OTHERS' VIEWS OF HOW TO LIVE

If you don't have goals and direction in your life, then you are really buying into other people's views of how to live. How? Because you lack the direction; you are greatly influenced by others and may not even realise it. Why not take control of your own direction in your life, and set some goals today?

## THE MORE SUCCESS, THE MORE CRITICISMS YOU WILL RECEIVE

One thing is true: the more success you have, the more criticisms you will receive. However, when you use objectivity both on the praise and the criticisms you receive, you will never let the criticisms of others affect you in a negative way. Remember, it is just part of the deal that comes along with success.

## BE RESPONSIBLE AND YOU'LL GET MORE HELP

Have you ever noticed that it is the most focused and responsible people who get the most help in life from others? People see the responsibility already taken, and feel good about lending a hand and helping out. It works the other way as well. People are always reluctant to help others who never take responsibility. Be responsible and attract the help you need.

A successful man is one who can build a firm foundation with the bricks that others throw at him.

*David Brinkley*

ALLOW
OTHERS TO
IMPACT YOU

ONLY IN THE
DIRECTION
OF YOUR
GOALS

## ALL'S WELL THAT BEGINS WELL

You have heard the expression that all's well that ends well. However, things that end up well usually also began well. How we begin an effort with our preparation can make all the difference between a good result and a bad result. Anything worth doing right is worth beginning with the right preparation.

## PUT YOURSELF IN A POSITION TO WIN

You can't win unless you put yourself in a position to win first. Putting yourself in a position to win means doing your preparation, developing the right skills and behaviours, and taking risks, thereby growing your courage to try what you currently think is impossible. Put yourself in a position to win.

## PRACTISE IT IN YOUR HEAD

Did you ever hear the story about the prisoner from the Vietnam War who spent his time in captivity playing 18 holes of golf on his home course every day in his head (hitting every shot perfectly)? After he was finally released and went home, he played a round of golf on his home course and played dramatically better than he ever did before (remember – he had not touched a golf club in many years). There is real power in practising in your head. Try it today.

## WHAT YOU PRACTISE, YOU BECOME

Some people think they will improve just by thinking about it. Thinking about something improves your focus, but you need to put in the practice to make it part of your normal behaviour and habits. Move from thinking to practice and see the difference in your performance.

## BE PREPARED WHEN THE BREAKS COME YOUR WAY

It is always unsuccessful people who complain that they never receive the 'breaks' that others receive. Successful people take a different attitude. They expect breaks to come their way, but also understand that they need to be prepared to take advantage of those breaks when they arrive. If you have not prepared when the breaks come your way, you will never be in a position to take advantage of them.

The secret of success in life is for a man to be ready for his opportunity when it comes.

*Benjamin Disraeli*

PREPARATION
OFTEN
SEPARATES

THE SUCCESSFUL
FROM THE
UNSUCCESSFUL

TIME TO GET *started*

## RECOVERY TIME – AN EXAMPLE OF WHY IT IS IMPORTANT

A lecturer, when explaining stress management, raised a glass of water and talked about its weight. He said, 'The absolute weight doesn't matter. It depends on how long you try to hold it.' If he holds it for a minute, that's not a problem. If he holds it for a day, you'll have to call an ambulance. That's the way it is with stress management. If we carry our burdens all the time, they become increasingly heavy and difficult to carry. That is why our recovery time is so important.

## PLAN YOUR RECOVERY TIME

All too often people say that they will do some type of recovery, either exercise or read a book, if they have the time. Well, the 'time' never comes unless you schedule it. Plan your recovery; you will keep stress in check and have enough time and energy for all your other commitments.

## THINK – RECHARGE AND RELOAD

It is important to 'recharge the batteries' in order to keep our energy level up and to relieve stress. Everyone has their own way to do this, but the important thing is to find your way, and as Nike says, 'Just Do It'. Also, it is important to find a way to 'reload the ideas' into yourself, which also gives you energy. A great way is reading, as it triggers new thoughts and ideas that give you energy in then trying to pursue them. Therefore, think each week – recharge the batteries and reload the ideas.

## MAKE RECOVERY OF EQUAL IMPORTANCE

Many times we say to ourselves, I am going to exercise, or go to the movies, etc. (some sort of recovery) if I can 'fit it in'. To keep our stress in check and have a more balanced life, we cannot treat recovery as a 'fit it in' activity. Recovery should be one of the activities that go into your calendar with the same importance as other key work projects, and other things should fit around them. Make recovery of equal importance in your life and you will feel less stressed.

## IT IS EASIER TO KEEP GOOD HEALTH THAN TO REGAIN IT

Being healthy and in good shape is on everyone's minds these days. Many people's weight goes up and down like a yo-yo. We forget that it is always easier to maintain good health than to regain it. We only need to put a few good habits in place and we can then keep that good health forever. What good habits could you put in place today?

The key to expanding capacity is to both push beyond one's ordinary limits and to regularly seek recovery, which is when growth actually occurs.

*Jim Loehr*

BALANCE
STRESS
WITH RECOVERY

TO KEEP
GROWING TO
YOUR
POTENTIAL

# TIME TO GET *started*

## YOUR REAL WEALTH IS BETWEEN YOUR EARS

Take any successful person and we could pinpoint the source of their wealth within five seconds. It is between their ears, and is shown to the outside world with their attitude and the discipline by which they live their life. To increase your wealth, look at developing yourself (between the ears).

## WHAT AM I BECOMING?

A good question to ask yourself is: 'What am I becoming?' To get more out of life, you need to become more (i.e. grow, to enable yourself to take on greater challenges). Ask yourself today, 'What am I becoming?' If the answer is not really what you want, then set some growth goals today and take action on them right away.

## YOUR BIGGEST PROBLEM IS YOU

If we are all honest, our biggest problem or barrier to success is ourselves. The same world is out there for everyone and all the opportunities are there. It is up to each of us to focus on what we want and develop ourselves to be the person who can get it. It's never anyone else who is preventing us getting what we want. It is just us!

## HOW CAN I IMPROVE?

Often, the questions we ask ourselves are what drives us to make the changes in our lives. Sometimes just a simple question such as 'How can I improve?' can create some great ideas on the ways to develop and the changes to make. Why not ask yourself today: 'How can I improve?'

## DON'T WISH IT WAS EASIER – WISH YOU WERE BETTER

Too often we all wish things were easier for us (e.g. work not so challenging, family issues not as difficult, etc.). However, instead of wishing things were easier, why don't we wish we were better? If we are constantly working on our own growth, we will find more things easier for us. What are your personal growth goals to become better?

Every achiever that I have ever met says, "My life turned around when I began to believe in me."
*Dr Robert Schuller*

WHEN YOU
BELIEVE
IN YOU

YOU BECOME
PART OF THE
SOLUTION

## HOW WELL IS YOUR FUTURE DEFINED?

Many people struggle to achieve what they want in life because they haven't defined it well enough. We all need to define our futures in such detail that it drives our daily actions and habits. If your desired future isn't driving your daily actions, you probably need to go back and define it in much more detail.

## SEEK OUT NEW CHALLENGES

People with passion will accomplish great things. However, how do they keep that passion alive? It is by seeking out new challenges that drives their passion to stay at high levels. If your passion is low, why not seek out some new challenges to keep your passion alive?

## IT IS THE JOURNEY AS WELL AS THE DESTINATION

Goals are very important, and having the future pictured in your mind is going to drive your actions. However, your life is about the way you get to your goals, as much as the achievement of those goals. Live your life in a way that you will be able not only to enjoy the achievement, but also the journey.

## PASSIVE HOPE TO ACTIVE EXPECTATION

Unsuccessful people are always hoping for a better future. They aren't taking any action towards it, so what they have is 'passive hope'. To be successful, you need to believe in yourself and expect a better future, and then take the action to make it happen. Build your life based on 'active expectation' from today.

## WE DON'T ASK FOR ENOUGH

Most people don't get all they can out of life because they are constantly playing it safe. You know, you can never get what you don't ask for. So, if you want more, you have to ask for more. However, the more you ask for, the stronger your personal development needs to be in order to become the type of person who can get it.

My interest is in the future because I am going to spend the rest of my life there.

*Charles Kettering*

TAKE INTEREST
IN YOUR
FUTURE

DEFINE
IT WELL AND
ENJOY
THE JOURNEY

## ALWAYS STRIVE TO IMPROVE YOUR COMMUNICATIONS

Much of what we accomplish is down to our ability to communicate with others. It's a core skill and we often don't take enough time to develop it. Take every opportunity to improve your communication skills and always treat it as one of the most important skills for your greater success.

## PEOPLE TUNE INTO INFORMATION IN DIFFERENT WAYS

People take in information in different ways. Some people are picture-oriented. They may say, 'I see what you mean.' Others are word-oriented and understand things better when powerful words are used. Try to explain your ideas to others in different ways. That way you have a better chance of connecting with everyone.

## COMMUNICATIONS – SAY IT, EXPLAIN IT, AND SAY IT AGAIN

Being a good communicator is a key skill in life, as everything we do involves communications with others. A good three steps to remember in communicating with others are the following: first, say it – what do you want to share? Then, explain it – provide more details and why it's important. And finally, say it again – repeat your key message. Follow these steps and you will be a more effective communicator.

## TELL PEOPLE THE COMMUNICATION METHOD YOU LIKE

Today, there are so many communication methods (phone, text, email, Skype, web messaging, etc.). Each of us has preferred methods for urgent and normal communications that match our working style. In order to be more productive, tell others which methods you prefer. Having people communicate with you in the method you prefer makes you more productive. But also remember, it goes both ways; so ask others their preferred communication methods as well and your communications to them will be better received and acted upon.

## THE POWER OF 'FOR EXAMPLE'

Have you noticed that people understand new concepts faster when you provide them with examples? You can also get other people's attention very quickly by using the words 'for example' in presentations and meetings. People begin to listen more closely when they hear the words 'for example', as examples are always more interesting to listen to than just information.

Communication skills are the lifeblood of a successful life... if you plan on spending any time there.

*Doug Firebaugh*

IMPROVE YOUR
LIFE
BY IMPROVING
YOUR
COMMUNICATION
SKILLS

TIME TO GET
*started*

## BUILD RELATIONSHIPS

A successful life is based on the relationships we have. They are key for business, as people prefer to do business with people they know and like. Relationships are key in our private lives, as they help us to grow and we are energised by the people we interact with. How strong are the relationships in your life?

## YOUR RELATIONSHIPS DRIVE YOUR SUCCESS

We all focus on getting things done and the 'Do'. However, our success is often more driven by the 'Who'. No-one is successful on his or her own, and it is the key relationships that we have developed that help us achieve our success. Before thinking 'Do', always think 'Who' could help. Also, think about helping others, as they will always in return help you.

## THE PEOPLE YOU WANT TO ATTRACT

The people you associate with will often determine the level of success you will achieve. For the success you desire, what type of people do you want to associate with, to attract? The more specific you are in whom you want to attract, the faster you will take the actions to attract those people.

## BUILD THE SOCIAL SKILLS FOR SUCCESS

The higher you climb in your career, it is always your social skills that enable your success the most. The ability to get in and out of difficult conversations in positive ways can be a big indicator of your success. Continue building your social skills and achieve even greater success.

## RELATIONSHIPS DRIVE OUR HAPPINESS

When we think about our lives, it is really the relationships that drive our happiness. Those family, friend and co-worker relationships drive the level of happiness in our lives. However, as in other things, we only get out what we put in. What have you put into your key relationships lately?

Entrepreneurs have two basic assets: their creativity and their relationships.

*Mark Victor Hansen*

# THE PATH
## TO SUCCESS

# IS BUILT
## UPON THE
### STRENGTH OF YOUR
# RELATIONSHIPS

## MOVE FROM 'HERE I AM' TO 'THERE YOU ARE'

Have you ever noticed that some people only want to talk about themselves? They are always saying to themselves, 'Here I am,' as their favourite subject is themselves. They need to move their internal dialogue to 'There you are' and change their focus to others. It is really much more interesting for you to know more about others, as you already know about yourself.

## COMPLETELY THERE FOR THEM

Listening and building trust with others is a very powerful way to gain friends, support, and help for what you want in life. When you are 'completely there' for others, you make them feel special and in return they will help you in any way they can. Remember, it all starts with you being completely there for them.

## TAKE THE FIRST STEP

Too often we develop problems with some people, and our first thoughts are to avoid them and so avoid the problem. This solution never works, and the problem never remains the same size – it only gets bigger. Be the one who takes the first step and talk to the other person. Be big enough to take the first step.

## MATCH BODY LANGUAGE FOR BETTER RAPPORT

If you want to influence and build a greater rapport with people, match their body language when having a meeting with them. If they are sitting straight, sit straight also. If they are sitting back in their chair, sit back as well. Do the opposite and you'll create a little tension without saying a word. Match body language in your next meeting.

## CAPTURE THE EXACT WORDS PEOPLE SAY

When taking notes in meetings, always capture the exact words that others say. Many people try to translate (paraphrase) their notes into their own way of saying it, but by doing this you lose the advantages. Capturing the exact words of others allows you to use their words back to them in emails or other communications. By using their exact words you have a much better way of gaining improved rapport, and influencing them.

There is a thread con-
necting you no matter
how far away you are
from someone, and you
know, I have two or three
relationships in my life
that are like that.

*P. J. Harvey*

YOUR
CONNECTIONS

WILL BE AS
STRONG
AS YOU MAKE THEM

## YOUR NETWORK CREATES YOUR NET WORTH

Charlie 'Tremendous' Jones always said that you will be the same five years from now except for two things: (1) the books you read, and (2) The people you meet. The people you meet (your network) are the ones who will help you grow and point out the opportunities for your success. You could say that your network will help grow your net worth. What is the quality of your network (i.e. the people you are meeting)?

## MAKE CONTACT, NOT JUST CONTACTS

People often try networking to grow their contacts, but don't really make 'contact'. They don't spend the quality time necessary to get to know each other better. It is only after you get to know each other well that you see opportunities that are of benefit to each other. So, make contact and not just contacts.

## FIRST IMPRESSIONS

First impressions are so important. People form an initial impression of you in the first 10 seconds of when you meet. Then, they take every interaction with you after that and compare it to that first impression. You can repair a bad first impression, but it takes multiple interactions with the other person before they realise that their initial impression was not the right one. Make sure you make the right first impression.

## BE SPECIFIC WITH YOUR COMPLIMENTS

Nothing motivates people more than sincere compliments. In fact, the more specific the compliments, the stronger the impact you will have on both the motivations and behaviours of others. So, be as specific as you can be with your compliments.

## GO ASK PEOPLE HOW THEY GOT THERE

A simple thing to do to increase your success is something most people never attempt. The truly successful people never did it on their own, and went to other successful people and asked how they got there. They found out the 'habits' of success. Why not offer to buy lunch for successful people you know and ask them the key habits and actions that got them where they are today?

Networking is an essential
part of building wealth.
*Armstrong Williams*

NETWORKING
IS ALL ABOUT

HELPING
EACH OTHER TO
BE EVEN MORE
SUCCESSFUL

## TWO EARS AND ONE MOUTH – USE THEM IN THAT PROPORTION

Often we talk too much and listen too little. You would think that the most pleasant sound to us is ourselves talking! Take the time to ask questions and listen more to others. You have to listen to learn more. Talking only helps you to make clear in your mind what you already know.

## LISTEN FIRST ALWAYS

Too often we go into a meeting with someone and all we want to do is to tell the other person how much we know. Fight this urge. Instead, ask questions first. It is much easier to convince someone or move them to your way of thinking by listening first. You can build upon their own thoughts in a way that supports your way of thinking. Listen first today.

## LISTEN AND PLAYBACK IN THEIR OWN WORDS

If you really want to influence someone, you need to listen first. Listen to their words, the way they express different thoughts and make note of the exact words and phrases they use. By using their words, packaged in a different way, you have a better chance of influencing them than just using your own words and ways of expressing thoughts. Therefore, to influence others – listen first.

## LISTENING AND PARAPHRASING

Having good listening skills is essential in business these days. If we listen well, we learn more and we build a better rapport with our co-workers and customers. One key skill in listening is paraphrasing. This involves saying back to the other person – in your own words – what he or she has been saying. By paraphrasing, you are showing the other person that you have been listening and that you understand what was said. You can't paraphrase unless you have understood it well enough to describe it in your own words. You also benefit as you will remember it better, as we always seem to remember better what we say.

## YOU LISTEN WITH YOUR EMOTIONS

We all take in more of what others say when we are not only interested in the subject, but if it also creates some emotion within us. We actually listen better when others engage us not just intellectually, but emotionally. That is why the best speakers are great storytellers. They engage our emotions.

Most people do not listen with the intent to under-stand; they listen with the intent to reply.

*Stephen R. Covey*

LISTENING
TO UNDERSTAND

MAKES ALL
THE DIFFERENCE

## TIME TO GET
## started

## KEEP PERSONALITIES IN MIND

Everyone has a different personality and way of working. For example, if you want to influence a direct and straight-talking manager, you don't use an indirect approach. You also speak very directly, and match the speed that he or she is talking. It is always important to adapt your style to match the person you are talking to.

## BE POSITIVE AND HAVE POWER TO INFLUENCE OTHERS

There's a big difference in people who are either negative or positive. Being negative doesn't attract others to you and they really don't want to listen to you. However, if you are positive, others want to be around you and will listen to you more. Remember, be positive and have the power to influence others.

## CONTENT AND CONTEXT

Content and context are two important words to remember when we see two people react in different ways to the same event. The content is what both people observe, but the context each person creates is based on their life experiences (which may be quite different). They will each apply a different meaning to the same event. Keep this in mind when you see others react to the same event in different ways, and consider their life experiences that have shaped their reaction.

## GET TO THE POINT

People are often not successful at influencing others because they do not get to the point fast enough. Influencing others has much to do with your preparation. If you prepare what you want to say and how, as well as possible questions or responses, you will have much higher success in influencing others. Do your preparation and get to the point faster.

## CAPTURE THE EXACT WORDS

When taking notes in meetings, always look to capture the exact words used by others. This allows you to use their exact words back to them in future emails and conversations. People respond better when you use their way of saying things and when you remember exactly what they said.

The greatest ability in business is to get along with others and to influence their actions.

*John Hancock*

TO INFLUENCE
OTHERS

FIRST SEEK TO
GAIN
RAPPORT

## RESPOND TO THE FEELINGS, THEN THE FACTS

Whenever you are engaged in a conversation filled with emotion, respond first to the feelings, then the facts. If you acknowledge the other person's feelings and make him or her more comfortable, they will be in a much better state to discuss (listen to) the facts.

## FEEL, FELT, FOUND

To help someone through an issue, use the 'feel, felt, found' approach. You can say: 'I understand how you feel. I have felt the same way in a similar situation. Could I share with you what I have found?' It is a powerful way to get others in a position to listen to your advice. Try it. It works.

## NEVER ARGUE FROM EXTREMES

It is important when arguing a point with others never to take an extreme position or provide an extreme example. People who make points from extremes do not really argue from a position of power, as anyone can find an extreme point in their favour in any argument. Remember: never argue from extremes or take an extreme position.

## CAN I MAKE A DISTINCTION?

When you are talking to a person who may take the opposite side of an issue that is important to you, why not ask permission to express your own thoughts (but in a very polite and non-confrontational way)? You could say, 'Can I make a distinction for you?' It is a good way to be able to introduce your own thinking. Then, you could follow up and say, 'This is what others have found' as well. Try this in the coming weeks when the situation arises.

## IF THE CUSTOMER IS TALKING, YOU ARE WINNING

There's an old saying in sales that if the customer is talking, you are winning. This is because the salesperson is asking open questions and is sincerely interested in the customer's business and how to help them make more profit. You can take the same approach to your personal relationships and strive to listen more than you talk.

Before you can inspire with emotion, you must be swamped with it yourself. Before you can move their tears, your own must flow. To convince them, you must yourself believe.

*Sir Winston Churchill*

TO CONVINCE
OTHERS

CONVINCE
YOURSELF
FIRST

## GOOD LEADERS KNOW WHO THEY ARE

Good leaders know who they are. They know their strengths and their weaknesses, and surround themselves with people who have strengths in their areas of weakness. This helps both the leader and his or her team to accomplish more, and it all starts with them knowing their own strengths and weaknesses well.

## LEADERSHIP REQUIRES ENTHUSIASM

A leader can never expect his or her people to act any differently from the way they act themselves. If you want your people to have enthusiasm, then you, as a leader, must act enthusiastically. Nothing generates action faster than an enthusiastic leader.

## LISTENING – THE FUEL FOR LEADERSHIP

One of the greatest skills for a leader to be more successful is the skill of listening. The more you listen, the more fuel (information) you get to find the right way to motivate your people.

## LEAD BY EXAMPLE

Most people learn more by observing others' behaviours than by listening to what they say. Leaders have a greater influence on others by their actions rather than by their words. As a leader, always think of leading by example and you will generate a much stronger impact on your people. What example do you provide now?

## PROBLEMS – DO THEY IMPACT STRENGTHS OR WEAKNESSES?

You can tell by observing problems and people's reactions to them whether the problems are in a person's strengths or weaknesses. If the problem is in a person's area of weakness, they will feel threatened by it and avoid the problem. If it is in the person's area of strength, they will draw energy to solve the problem and solve it quickly.

Leadership is the art of getting someone else to do something you want done because he wants to do it.

*Dwight D. Eisenhower*

LEADING
IS TRANSFERRING
YOUR
ENTHUSIASM

TO YOUR
PEOPLE

TIME TO GET
*started*

## LEAD WITH QUESTIONS, NOT ANSWERS

To lead people to take their own initiative, you need to lead with questions and not answers. Ask your people the questions that will help them think through their problems and opportunities. They will begin to see the answers themselves and build their own confidence up so that they can think of the right questions and answers on their own next time. Remember: questions, not answers.

## NEVER SAVE YOUR PEOPLE FROM THINKING

Leaders are always busy, and when their people come to them with problems, they sometimes just simply give them the answer. What those leaders have done is saved their people from thinking. It is better to ask questions in such a way that their people see the answers.

## WHAT OPTIONS DO YOU THINK WE HAVE?

A great question to use as a leader is: 'What options do you think we have?' Whenever issues or problems arise, the most effective way is to ask your people for their opinions. You can also ask: 'What do you think we should do?' However, I have found that asking for options works best. It encourages a real dialogue on the different options, and better ideas come up. Asking your people helps them to feel more ownership of the solution and can make the implementation of it much smoother. So, why not ask your people today, 'What options do you think we have?'

## HELP OTHERS THINK THINGS THROUGH

One of the best things a leader can do is to help his or her people think things through. When a leader helps their people to see the answer in themselves, two things happen: (1) the people get the confidence that they can do it again – maybe by themselves next time; and (2) they know they have the support of the leader – who helped them think it through.

## HOW CAN I GET THE BEST FROM YOU?

A great goal for a leader is to get the best from each of their people. So, why not ask them: 'How can I get the best from you?' You will be surprised at how open and honest they will be on what motivates them, and just how powerful their ideas can be to you as their leader.

The important thing is
not to stop questioning.
*Albert Einstein*

IT'S THE
QUESTIONS

THEY HAVE
THE 'TRUE'
POWER

## THE ABILITY TO RECOGNISE ABILITY

One of the most important abilities in a leader is the ability to recognise ability. Great leaders build a winning team around them. They not only recognise the ability in others, but also know how to use it to the fullest for the good of the team. How is your ability to recognise ability?

## AS GOOD AS THE PEOPLE AROUND YOU

Look at many of today's business or government leaders and you will notice something interesting. Very often these leaders are as good (effective) as the people around them. Great leaders all have one trait in common. They are great at picking people for their team.

## NEVER COMPROMISE WHEN PICKING PEOPLE

Very often there is a great pressure to add the necessary resources, and we compromise on our selection because of the time pressure. Compromises never work in the long run, as we end up having the wrong people on board and difficulty getting rid of them. Never compromise when picking people.

## HIRE PEOPLE WHO ARE GOOD AT WHAT YOU ARE NOT

The best managers hire people to do things they are not good at. It is important to know your strengths, but equally important to understand your own weaknesses. Spend your time fully utilising your strengths, and you will accomplish more. Then, hire people to do things in your area of weakness, and you now have a very powerful combination.

## WHEN IN DOUBT, DON'T HIRE – KEEP LOOKING

We sometimes look at candidates for jobs and ask ourselves the question, 'Could I live with that?' Something in the person's behaviour makes us ask that question. If we are asking the question, then we need to think seriously about whether this person is right for our company. Experience shows us that behaviour issues observed during the interview process are always worse in the real work life. When in doubt, don't hire. Keep looking.

The best leader is the one who has sense enough to pick good people to do what he/she wants done, and self-restraint enough to keep from meddling with them while they do it.

*Theodore Roosevelt*

SURROUND
YOURSELF

WITH THE BEST
PEOPLE
AVAILABLE

## DELEGATE TO GROW YOUR PEOPLE FASTER

People sometimes forget this, but delegating is the most effective way to grow your people. It is also a double win. Your people grow faster as they quickly learn what they need to know in order to do the delegated task. Learning and growing faster is very motivating for them. You benefit by having the job done by someone else and get a stronger person in the process. All they need is a little coaching upfront.

## LOOK FOR PERSONAL COMMITMENT

In looking at any new initiative, always look for the personal commitment from the people you will be dealing with. Success for any initiative comes down to the level of personal commitment from everyone, and if the personal commitment is low, the results will be the same.

## STRETCH YOUR PEOPLE WITH NEW CHALLENGES

Your people grow faster when new challenges are given to them. Training helps to provide the knowledge and foundation, but it is the new challenges and experiences that put the training to good use and develop your people faster. Look for new challenges for your people this week.

## HELP YOUR PEOPLE WITH THEIR OWN DECISION MAKING

Delegating to your people means delegating some decision making as well. It is important to help your people make decisions by asking questions to help them think through the issues. Your questions have two purposes: (1) questions show them the way to think through issues in order to have the right information to make the decisions; (2) the experience with your help shows them a way then to help their own people.

## EMPOWERMENT LEADS TO 'OWNERSHIP'

Empowerment is talked about a great deal these days. It is important to empower your people to use their own initiative and make decisions. However, the real 'power' in empowerment is that people then take ownership for their areas of responsibility. Ownership, now that's the real power.

Delegating means letting others become the experts and hence the best.
*Timothy Firnstahl*

DELEGATING
IS THE FASTEST WAY TO GROW YOUR PEOPLE

## NOT RESPONSIBLE FOR, BUT RESPONSIBLE TO

Sometimes managers feel that they are responsible for their people. They take everything on themselves and feel personally impacted by the actions and feelings of their people. Your people need to feel responsible for their own lives, and as their manager you are not responsible for, but responsible to, them. Your responsibility is to create an environment in which they can develop and succeed. It is up to them to take advantage of that environment and then to make it happen.

## GIVE PEOPLE A VISION OF WHAT IS POSSIBLE

People will sometimes amaze you with what they accomplish. If we, as leaders, constantly provide a vision of what is possible, our people will turn those possibilities into reality. What would you accomplish if someone was constantly telling you what is possible for you?

## INVEST QUALITY TIME WITH YOUR BEST PEOPLE

Great leaders invest a large proportion of their time with their best people. They don't let their problem people drain away the time that is available for their best people. This way they are helping their best people grow faster and that helps the company to grow faster as well. How much time do you invest with your best people?

## WORK AROUND THE WEAKNESSES OF YOUR PEOPLE

Trying to turn around major weaknesses in your people can be almost impossible sometimes (especially if your people don't buy into changing). One way is to work around their weaknesses. Focus on using their strengths to the maximum and find others to fill the gaps caused by their weaknesses. Focusing on everyone's strengths and utilising them the best way you can will help you to grow the strongest organisation possible.

## CREATE MENTORS IN YOUR ORGANISATION

Mentors are a good way to grow your organisation. A mentor can have a different relationship with the employee than the boss can have. Some subjects can be addressed by a mentor that can make a huge difference in the performance of the employee being mentored. Ask for a mentor for yourself today, and speed your personal development and growth.

People grow through experience if they meet life honestly and courageously. This is how character is built.
*Eleanor Roosevelt*

# EXPAND
## EXPERIENCES &
## RESPONSIBILITIES

AND SEE THE
GROWTH
IN YOUR PEOPLE

## MAKE YOUR PEOPLE ACCOUNTABLE

As a leader, it is important that your people feel accountable for their areas of responsibilities. When they bring problems to you, don't solve the problems for them. Instead, ask questions to help them find solutions on their own. That way the accountability for implementing solutions does not fall back on you.

## WHERE IS THE AUTHORITY AND ACCOUNTABILITY?

In large companies today there are many matrix organisations, and most have a big problem with authority and accountability all over the place. The more you can focus authority and accountability in the same leader and group, the more change you can drive and in a much more consistent way.

## ALWAYS FOLLOW UP THE COMMITMENTS OF OTHERS

It is important always to follow up the commitments made to you by others, for three reasons: (1) you make sure they get their commitment done on time so as not to impact adversely on your own productivity; (2) you reinforce good behaviours in others (they notice you follow up); (3) your credibility increases as people will respect you more (they see you are very organised).

## YOU GET THE BEHAVIOURS YOU REINFORCE

As a leader, it is always important to follow up on the commitments of your people. If you follow up, you reinforce the good behaviours of keeping commitments, and if you don't follow up, you reinforce something else. Remember, you get the behaviours you reinforce.

## REWARD THE DOERS

You see it all too often in large organisations: people are being rewarded for strategies and plans, but not the doing. This is changing now, but the best way to improve an organisation and its culture is to reward the doers. How are your reward structures set up in your company?

Accountability     breeds
response-ability.
*Stephen R. Covey*

WHEN PEOPLE
ARE HELD
ACCOUNTABLE

THEY DO WHAT IS
NECESSARY
TO DELIVER

## SAVE TIME IN MEETINGS: 'WHAT'S THE SUCCESSFUL OUTCOME?'

At the beginning of meetings, ask the question: 'What's the successful outcome of this meeting?' or 'What do we want to accomplish?' This helps to keep everyone focused on the goal of the meeting and for the conversations to stay focused as well. For your next meeting, ask the question: 'What's the successful outcome?'

## DO THE PREP FOR YOUR MEETINGS

How many times do we go into our meetings unprepared? Too often! The minimum is to have an agenda that will meet the goal of your meeting (the successful achievement of_____?) The prep done means that the goal of the meeting is defined, the right people will be there, and you know well the position of everyone coming into the meeting (if you want to drive a decision in the meeting). Do the prep for your next meeting and make it a very successful meeting.

## ORGANISE YOUR FACE-TO-FACE MEETINGS

Too often we get our people together for a face-to-face meeting and force them to listen to PowerPoint® presentation after PowerPoint® presentation. Just sharing information can be done in many other ways. Use your face-to-face meetings for more teamwork activities and organise people into smaller groups to attack your major issues with discussions, not PowerPoints®.

## BRAINSTORM USING POST-IT® NOTES

An excellent way to brainstorm with your team is to give everyone Post-it® notes to write down their ideas. You can then put all the ideas up on the wall and arrange them into categories. When you see all the ideas together, you suddenly see even more ideas. There is something about the physical act of writing and rearranging Post-it® notes that brings more creativity and more ideas.

## KNOW YOUR AUDIENCE (PARTICIPANTS)

When running a meeting, it is really important to know your participants (i.e. what is their position on the subject and how will they act in the meeting?). When you are running a meeting, you are like an orchestra conductor. You want some participants to speak up more and others less (even to shut up!). How you manage the participants can be the difference between having a successful meeting or not.

When the result of a meeting is to schedule more meetings, it usually signals trouble.

*Kevin Murphy*

# SUCCESSFUL MEETINGS HAVE CLEAR OUTCOMES

## AND THE RIGHT PREPARATION & PARTICIPANTS

TIME TO GET
started

### LEADING A TEAM – DRIVE INTERDEPENDENCE

When leading a team, especially a 'virtual team' (where people are located at different sites), it is often a good idea to drive interdependence. This means to give a responsibility to each key team member to drive something for the entire team. It could be to develop a new process or to solve a particular problem that everyone has. What's important is that each key member must work with the others to be successful, and each key member has their own project as well. So, they will really need to help and support each other to be successful. They need to depend on each other.

### CREATE WAYS FOR YOUR PEOPLE TO KNOW EACH OTHER BETTER

It is valuable to find ways for your people to get to know each other better. Teams with members who know each other well perform better than other teams. Each of the team members better understands the others' personalities and there are fewer problems with misinterpreting each other's behaviours. That is why it is important to organise external activities. These can be social events, or sports such as volleyball, go-karting, football, etc. Think about how you can get your team knowing each other better.

### USE THE POWER WITHIN YOUR TEAM

There are too many meetings where the same people in your team do all the talking, and they probably don't have the best ideas all the time. Find ways to get input from the whole team. Have everyone write their ideas on Post-it® notes, and share all the ideas before having the discussion. This helps you to use the full power within your team.

### YOU NEED DEBATE IN YOUR TEAM

To build a highly effective team, you have to have some debate over issues. Diversity in teams (in terms of thinking, personalities, etc.) makes them stronger, and these teams usually come up with more creative and better solutions. Create a diverse team and give them the opportunities to debate the issues.

### SHARE SUCCESSES WITHIN THE TEAM

It is a good idea to have a section in your team meetings to share the week's or month's successes. People like to talk about how they have been successful, and others often get ideas about how they could do something similar in their area. Also, sharing successes creates energy in the room, and a great time to do it is right before looking at future opportunities for the team.

A team is a group of people who may not be equal in experience, talent, or education but in commitment.

*Patricia Fripp*

SUCCESSFUL
TEAMS
HAVE COMMITMENT

TO THE OUTCOMES
AND TO EACH
OTHER

## THE RATE OF CHANGE INSIDE YOUR ORGANISATION

Jack Welch made a really telling statement: 'When the rate of change inside your organisation is less than the rate of change outside your organisation, the end is in sight.' This is important not just for organisations, but for individuals as well (and especially for leaders). It is always important to keep growing as leaders so that you can continue to pass on your knowledge and abilities to help grow others. The key question is then: what's the rate of change inside you?

## FREEDOM AND RESPONSIBILITY WITHIN A FRAMEWORK

The very best companies provide an environment where their people have the freedom to make decisions. These companies very clearly outline the key principles and processes to work within, and then allow their people to make things happen. The framework is there to clearly define the responsibility that the people can take.

## ORGANISATIONS GROW TO THE LIMITS OF THEIR LEADERS

If you really want to grow your organisation, then concentrate on growing your leaders first. Leaders cannot lift people to higher levels of performance if they are not growing themselves at a faster pace. Therefore, grow your leaders in order to grow your organisation.

## CUSTOMERS DETERMINE THE CULTURE YOU NEED

Many leaders are focused on the culture they need to drive in their companies to be successful. However, often they take a too internal view on this and miss their most important source – their customers. Remember, it is your customers that determine the culture you need.

## THINK ABOUT THE 'CUSTOMER EXPERIENCE'

Too often we worry only about the end result of our service to our customers. However, customers evaluate us on all of what we do, and form their impressions by the sum total of all their interactions with us (i.e. the Total Customer Experience). Make it a goal of your organisation to make every customer interaction a positive experience.

Any organization will be only as successful as those at the bottom are willing to make it.
*General Bill Creech*

ALL SUCCESSFUL
ORGANISATONS
HAVE
EVERYONE

FEELING INVOLVED
IN DELIVERING THE
CUSTOMER
EXPERIENCE

## TIME TO GET *started*

## EVERY LEADER IS IN 'SHOW' BUSINESS

If you think about it, every leader is really in 'show' business. They are always communicating to their people to 'show' the direction and the possibilities for their organisation's success. Also, they are the 'show' in many cases, as they are their people's role model. Remember, as a leader you are in 'show' business.

## BE A ROLE MODEL

People don't always remember this, but everyone sees everything. People notice how we work, how we interact with each other, and how we speak of others in their absence. Remember, our actions speak louder than our words. Always strive to live as the role model you would like to be.

## IMPRESS UPON, NOT JUST TO IMPRESS

There are many people who try to impress others with their talents and abilities, and are usually just trying to feed their egos. However, the people with real power set a goal to impress upon others. They want to set a good example and be a great role model. Their goal is to impress upon others, versus just to impress.

## ROLE MODELS – THE MOST POWERFUL WAY TO EDUCATE

The most powerful way to educate others is by being the best role model you can be. People notice everything a leader does, and by observing the leader's habits, they pick them up for themselves (whether they are good habits or bad habits!). It is important to make sure your people pick up good habits, so be the best role model you can be.

## WANT OTHERS TO DEVELOP? DEVELOP YOURSELF

If you really want to develop your people, start with developing yourself first. You cannot develop your people effectively unless you are developing at a faster pace than your people. Your development (learnings and experiences) is the best source of development for your people, as they have an excellent role model in front of them every day. At what pace is your development?

A leader is one who knows the way, goes the way and shows the way.
*John Maxwell*

# A LEADER
## SHOWS THE WAY

# BY WHO THEY ARE AND HOW THEY ACT

### MARK FRITZ

Mark is the founder of the thriving company Procedor, and has for years successfully combined best practices from around the world to create an innovative set of business tools and insights that can help businesses of all sizes to be successful. Mark is an associate of Ashridge College in the UK, co-teaching Leading Complex Teams, and leads an MBA Seminar on Virtual Leadership at HEC in France. He also leads MBA workshops on Virtual Leadership at the Instituto de Empresa Business School in Spain.

Mark's natural charm and personable style, enhanced by a great sense of humour, make him a speaker of choice at company events and seminars; he is also an affiliate of the prestigious CSA Celebrity Speakers.

In the upcoming year Mark will publish several books, one of which will be in the same series as *Time to Get Started*. *Every Week is a New Beginning* is the next step in both your personal and professional life, to give you the tools to get where you want to be.

"This book (*Every Week is a New Beginning*) is presented in a clear, concise and accessible way with bite-sized 'golden nuggets' aimed chiefly at the convenience of the reader rather than presenting the usual homilies found in many management books. I commend it to you."

Anton Ratnayake BSc, MCMI, WCIT